From Sunrise to Sunset
A Poetic Journey

Nashanta Taylor-Weems

Copyright © 2012 Nashanta Taylor-Weems

All rights reserved.

(Tranquil Moments Publishing)

ISBN-13: 978-0988279469
ISBN-10: 0988279460

DEDICATION

This book is dedicated to everyone that believed in me and gave me the strength, courage and faith to follow my dreams, but is not here to share in it with me. To my mother, Elder Diane Weems and my grandmother, Pearl Smith; two of the strongest women I knew. They filled me with the courage, the strength and the power to trust God and follow my dreams. My dad, Elder Roy Weems Sr., my grandfather, Andrew Smith Sr. and my uncle, Andrew Smith Jr.; these men showed me what a man, a father and a husband is meant to be. And lastly, to my godparents; Pastor and Mrs. Clarence Lobdell and Mr. and Mrs. Elbert Spencer and all my other loved ones that have gone on to glory, thank you all for blessing my life with whatever role that you played in it, I hope that I am making you proud.

Sincerely,
Nashanta Taylor-Weems

CONTENTS

	Acknowledgments	i
1	From Sunrise, To Sunset	Pg 1
2	Why Am I Here?	Pg 2
3	And God Answers	Pg 3
4	To The One	Pg 4
5	The Past	Pg 5
6	Friends	Pg 6
7	Never Ending Love Song Pt. 1 and 2	Pg 8
8	Why Can't You See Me?	Pg 10
9	You (The Stranger)	Pg 11
10	What Are You Feeling	Pg 12
11	What Do You See? (Watching Me?)	Pg 13
12	Dreaming	Pg 14
13	What Is It About You?	Pg 15
14	One Day	Pg 16
15	When Does My Heart Mend?	Pg 17
16	Turn Your Back	Pg 18
17	Time	Pg 19
18	This Is ME	Pg 20
19	One Last Letter	Pg 21
20	Just Let Her Be	Pg 22

21	It's Not That Easy	Pg 23
22	It Ain't The First Time	Pg 24
23	I Wanna Be Loved	Pg 25
24	Now That It's Over	Pg 26
25	The End	Pg 27
26	Suicide	Pg 28
27	Society	Pg 31
28	Sex and Sports	Pg 33
29	Reality Check	Pg 35
30	Not Enough Tine	Pg 36
31	Love = Music	Pg 37
32	I'll Take My Time, We'll Take It Slow	Pg 38
33	I Knew That It Would Never Work	Pg 40
34	Hitmaker	Pg 41
35	Have You Ever Loved?	Pg 43
36	Gone Too Soon	Pg 44
37	Ex-Lovers Trying To Be Friends	Pg 47
38	Don't Cry For Me – For the Servicemen and Women	Pg 48
39	Dear Mama	Pg 49
40	Center Of My Life	Pg 50
41	Captivated	Pg 51
42	Behind These Brown Eyes	Pg 52

43	A Mother	Pg 53
44	A Chance	Pg 54
45	Now How Does It Feel?	Pg 55
46	Rape	Pg 56
47	Siblings	Pg 58
48	About the Author	Pg 62

ACKNOWLEDGMENTS

I first want to THANK and PRAISE GOD for allowing me to complete my book. This has been a long process for me but I am so blessed to see it completed and to be able to share my story with others. To Pastor Anthony Goffin Sr., thank you for being the Man of God that you are. At one of the lowest points in my life, God brought you to me. You guided me back to God and kept me grounded and for that I will be eternally grateful.

To my siblings; Joey, Tony, Uwanda, 'Sluggo', Chuck, Phay, Toni, Courtney, Michael, Marqus, Tamiko, and Chelsey, I love you all!!! But to my big sister who from the time I was brought home, up until the time she left home we fought, Joshica, I love you and would not trade you for the world. Through the good and the bad I never stopped looking up to you and wanting to be like my sister, "The Homecoming Queen." Thank you for being there for me. To ALL my other adoptive siblings (there are WAY too many of you guys to name) and sister/brother in-laws thank you for believing in me. To my dad, Norris Taylor, thank you for giving me life, it has not been easy but with God we have been able to move forward. To ALL my aunts, uncles and cousins in Smith, Weems and Taylor families I LOVE YOU and I am TRULY BLESSED to have you in my life! To my big cousins; Andrew III, Tara, Tammy, Reggie, Rodney and Renee, growing up with you guys there was never a dull moment. They say cousins are the first friends that you make, well as the baby with friends like you guys; there was no place for enemies. Just kidding, I love you all. To my cousin Ricki, it was a blessing to have you around, especially during my college years and the years after; you just don't know how many times you saved my life.

To Pastor and Lady Chivanda Goffin and the ENTIRE True Faith family…man I love you to LIFE!!! In my ministry and my personal life, I have grown so much being around you guys. The love that we share is truly a blessing; I could not be any more blessed with such a loving church and Pastor. But, I can't forget my roots; New Hope Missionary Baptist Church, where it all started. To my New Hope family, whether you are still there or not, may God continue to bless and keep you all!

To Crystal Best, where do I begin? You have been; a stylist, friend, confidant, mother, and so many other things to me. You have even been the editor for this book! Everything, that I have brought to you, no matter if you agreed with it or not, you supported me and I thank you for that, LOVE YOU CHICA!!! To Mindy and the rest of the Talley/Best family, thank you all for opening not just your homes but your hearts to me.

The Bible only promises us one maybe two REAL FRIENDS, I am blessed to have two! 20 plus years is a LONG time and if God allows it, 20 plus more years!! Kyla and Romel, when God made you two, He definitely had me in mind! I love you both and appreciate the love, support, and tough love you have shown me over the years!

To my publisher and business partner, Jahzara, girl you know that you were a God sent!! To this day, I still don't know how we met but we have been going strong in the Lord, building each other up and making our dreams our reality! Thank you for being a blessing and role model to me. May God continue to bless and keep you!

To everyone else that has crossed my path, I thank you as well. Please do not take it to heart if your name was not mentioned, you played a role in my life and making this book come full circle! I LOVE YOU!

And finally, I want to say thank you to you, the reader. Thank you for purchasing my book. I pray that through my experiences, you will see that you are not alone and that you can overcome ANYTHING if you keep God first. May God Bless you All!

1
FROM SUNRISE, TO SUNSET

Sunrises and sunsets have always been my favorite; I have enjoyed them for as long as I can remember. Sunrises and sunsets are the beginning and ending of day, the beginning and ending of a journey; it was only fitting for this to be the title of my first book.

I loved living by the beach, the open space made the perfect horizon. I am so amazed how the sun can be setting on one side but it is still bright on the other. In the evening, I would sit on my balcony and watch the sky change colors as the sun goes down.

Each day brings a new test, each night a time of rest. The blue and yellow colors on the clearest morning are just as amazing as the orange and purple hues on a winter's night.

When I think about my life and how things have come and gone, I know that there was for a reason; the sun had to set for something old to end just like the sun had to rise for something new to begin.

A sunset and a sunrise can bring a sense of peace; it is either the beginning of a new adventure or an ending to a day you don't want to ever see again.

I can go on and on about the beauty of sunrises or sunsets, but unless you go out and experience it for yourself, they will be only words.

2
WHY AM I HERE?

I've been beaten, lied on, talked about and mistreated. WHY AM I HERE?

I've been abused, neglected and my heart broken into pieces…WHY AM I HERE?

Everyone I love has either died or didn't love me back…WHY AM I HERE!?!?!?!

I'm oddly shaped and no matter what I do or try, my body still disgusts me…..GOD WHY AM I HERE!!!

I have battled with drugs and alcohol…
I have tried to do right but always coming up short….WHY AM I HERE?!?!

I have had one failed relationship after another,
I use to think it was them but 10 years later and I'm still alone.

I found myself questioning and thinking maybe it's me and asking "Why am I here?"

I have tried to kill myself twice, I can't even do that right….WHY AM I HERE?!?!

I have spent days and nights asking God to just take me out of my misery. And because I'm still here I now question if there really is a God….WHY AM I HERE?

WHY AM I HERE?!?!

3
AND GOD ANSWERS….

You asked why are you here many times and I heard you each time
You are here for a divine purpose; I've spared your life so you can help others.
You were created in my image so therefore you are beautiful no matter how big or small you are.

You asked why are you here…you are here because I have a greater destiny for you to fulfill.

I did not create you to fulfill the desires of the world, but I created you to rise above what the world says.

The people you have loved that are now at rest have fulfilled the I work I called them to do and it was time for them to come home.

For the ones you say that you have loved and they didn't love you back, "Think, was it really love or lust?"

I made you strong. The things I allowed you to see and endure were never meant to hurt you but to build you and make you stronger for the things to come.

My love for you is greater than you will ever know or could imagine.

Why are you here, you ask….
You are here because Greater is He that is in you, then he that is in the world.
When you are weak, it is My strength and mercy that keeps you.
You are not here by mistake or accident.

Why are you here you ask….
You are here to be a living testimony.

4
TO THE ONE

THIS GOES OUT TO THE ONE WHO GOD HAS PLACED IN THIS WORLD JUST FOR ME.....

I may not be the prettiest woman in the world, but I'm not ugly
I may not be the smartest woman, but I am not the dumbest either
I may not be the smallest woman and I may not be the biggest woman
My hair may not be the shortest or the longest
I may not even be the lightest or the darkest woman
BUT I am the woman that God has made just for you.

It was all those things that I am not that brought you to me.
I may not be the model chick that parades in XXL magazine,
But I am that MODEL chick that God had in mind when He was thinking about you and your rib.

I am not going to change to fit into the world standards, but I will change for the better.

I am the things that you never thought you wanted but God said that you needed.
My worldly imperfections are perfection in your eyes.
Could it be that opposites really do attract?
NAH, cause physical features and superficial desires fade away with time...
BUT ME, I am like a fine wine.... I only get BETTER with time.

So go ahead, continue to waste your time with the superficial things of life
I will be waiting, 'because you were made me for me and I for you.

If we have already met, your blinders are soon to come off.
No flashy cars or stereotypes can stop what God has ordained.
And if we have not yet met, it is soon to come because MY TIME is NOW!

5
THE PAST

You make me wonder about myself. Something about you seems to get to me. I sit and wonder about how things between us used to be and then I see how we are now and wonder if our past changed the way we could have been.

We let ignorance and lust get the best of us and in the way. Now we must pay the highest price of all, just being friends.

If I could turn back the hands of time, I swear that I would do things differently. Since I can't I must bear the difference and the pain that I have brought upon myself. Oh how I pray that one day we could truly be just friends, but our past keeps making it hard to do.

The love I have for you is true, but I will never know how true…for the past has taken that away from you, from me, from us.

Now I may never know if you could ever feel the same about me. I may never know if there could have ever been us, a true us, a genuine us.

6
FRIENDS

What is a friend? A friend is an angel from God.

A friend is someone who will love you through the good and the bad. Who will correct you and tell you when you are wrong, no matter if you get mad.

A true friend raids your refrigerator, goes through your closets just to see what is new. A real friend wouldn't care what your place looks like, they would simply say, "Girl what the heck happened in here? Looks like a tornado ran through:" all while picking things up and putting them where they belong.

A true friend tells you the truth when you ask 'How does this look?' A real friend wouldn't let you walk around all day with your shirt on backwards, just maybe the first hour. ☺

When it comes to friends true and real can sometimes be one in the same. When it comes to a true real friend, you can argue like it is the beginning of World War III and then five minutes later forget whatever the whole thing was about. You all cross each other, but no one else better come in between.

When it comes to friendship, it is not always about whom you have known the longest; sometimes it comes down to who has been there when you needed it the most.

A friend is someone whose shoulder you can cry on, but if you are crying because of something you did, get ready 'cause a real friend will tell you about yourself later.

Growing up I really never knew what true friendship was about. I tried to buy friendship and I did different things trying to fit in and hoped to be liked. It was not until I got older that I realized what friendship was all about. If you have a true friend, they will accept you for who you are and not for what you have or don't have.

Over the years I called many people 'friend,' but after I learned what the real meaning of friend was, I am blessed to say that I have two true and real friends. You can say that they are my BFF's. I love these two to life and do not take them for granted.

Through the good and the bad, my dumb moments they have been there. From the 'I told you so' or 'you know good and well you should not have done that,' they have corrected me in love. Some of the saddest, funniest, 'never would do again' moments have been spent with these two. The times we have shared, some of them feel like they were straight out of a movie; I have my Golden Girl and my Bad Boy; the best of both worlds. And whoever says that men and women cannot be just friends, you are wrong.

If at any point in time, I have called you friend or vice versa, know that I got nothing but love for you. And that throughout my life, you have made a difference and have helped shape me into the women that I am today.

THANK YOU FOR BEING A FRIEND!!!

7
NEVER ENDING LOVE SONG PT. 1 AND 2

I want your fingers to play me as if I were your personal piano.
I want every stroke to be the sweetest note to my heart.

Every day will be a new melody,
Every moment be a new verse

Even our crescendo times are a chorus for our never ending love song. Your love is like a melody that I have played in my mind over and over times before. Our love will truly be the song that doesn't end...

When we think the song is about to end it will start over again.
With every beat of my heart I will love you.

Even with the last beat, our love song will continue to play on through the children that were created from the love song that was almost never written.

When I met you I thought my love song was finally about to be written.

But instead it was just another rough draft gone wrong.

The sound that played in my heart and mind was as sweet as the sound of a hummingbird on a clear summer's day.

But now all I hear is a never ending train wreck.

I sit and wonder where and when we fell out of sync.

Why did we miss a beat...How did we miss a beat?

Instead of you playing me like I was your personal piano, you played me like a game...a game that I lost.

Sometimes I can still feel your heart beat when I lay on the spot where your chest once laid.

Since you have been gone what once used to be a sweet melody has turned into nothing but sour notes and off key strokes.

In the beginning EVERYTHING felt so in sync and in tune.

Now things seem so out of whack, like a needle playing on a scratched record.

EVERYTHING in me is still saying that you are my composer and it may even take several more rewrites before this song becomes a masterpiece.

I guess I'll just sit back and wait 'til you are ready to make the music of my heart and play the tracks of my love.

Image courtesy of Herman Trass

8
WHY CAN'T YOU SEE ME?

Why can't you see me for me? I don't wear weave and my breast are real.
I'm not a size 2, nor do I want to be.

Why can't you see me?

Are you so blinded by what the world says is beautiful that you can't see what real beauty is?

In a few years that "dime" that you thought was so fine is gonna start looking like a bad piece of swine.

When you realize that the only reason you married her was for her looks, you turn astray and commit sinful acts with no take backs.

Why can't you see me?

9
YOU (THE STRANGER)

You are someone who I don't know, but would like to get to know.
You have eyes that sparkle like the stars at night and a smile that is so bright that it lights up the darkest room.

You have hands that work all day, but I believe can caress all night.
You have an attitude that gives me gratitude just too even know your name.
You have this boyish, shy guy demeanor, but I see past that and hands down you are all man.

I may be older, but age ain't nothing but a number because my breath has been taken away by you.

You have tapped into something inside of me that no stranger has ever touched before. You are educated and dedicated; I hope you are not dedicated to someone else because I would like to be that someone.

You keep your composure even though I know you were caught off guard.
You stand tall, not just in stature but in personality and character.

You compliment me with sincerity and honesty.
You are genuine, unique unlike anybody else that I have met.

Maybe it is that Cali mentality or maybe it's just the way you are, but that is what I want to know… who you are, stranger?

10
WHAT ARE YOU FEELING?

One minute you want me around. The next minute you want me gone.
First you need me and can't do anything without me, and then you'd rather
deal with things alone than have me around.

What are you feeling?

You tell me you want me gone and things are not working between us. Do
you really want me gone? You tell me you have too much going on and I
just maximize your problems. Is that what you really feel?

Is having me not around really going to make things better for you?
If that's what you feel, then I will go.

I guess I never meant anything to you for you to let me go so easy.
I guess everything that you told me you were feeling was lies and what you
really feel for me is nothing.

11
WHAT DO YOU SEE? (WATCHING ME)

As you stand and look down at me, what do you see in me?
Do you say to yourself, "That could have been my queen if we only had taken the right path?"

As you watch me day after day, do you still see me the same way from the first time we met?

When you look at me, can you see yourself in me? Am I your reflection?
Watching me every day do you see the pain that I am trying to hide?

Can you still read me just by looking at me?
Can you finish my sentence?

Do you see your future queen?
Or do you still see the whore that I was we when use to have sex?

Tell me what do you see when you look at me?
Do you see my love?
Do you see my pain?

As we stand together one last time, you watch me walk away.
Do you have any more to say?

What are you thinking; maybe one last kiss, maybe one last try?
No, I have cried my last cry, I think it is time to say goodbye.

So as you watch me walk away, what do you see?
I will tell you what you see…

You see woman who thought she would die if you were not there.
But now since years have passed, I am still here.

So as you watch me walk away for the very last time, know that it is for the best

12
DREAMING

Growing up as a kid and even to this day, I had a vivid imagination; always dreaming about something. I dreamed of being like the people on TV; I dreamed I had a TV life, you know how everything is better after thirty or sixty minutes.

I dreamed about my graduation day and how I would look in my cap and gown. I dreamed what my life would be like when I got older. I dreamed, of marriage and children, a big house and a car.

I dreamed of what and who I would be when I grew up.
But what I didn't dream was the life that I was actually going to have; this life God could have come up with.

The dreams that I dreamt are now becoming reality and it is far better than I could have ever imagined. I have realized that no matter how old you get, it is never too late to make your dreams a reality. A dream will only remain a dream if you don't put in the work. If God gave it to you, believe that it is going to come to pass, but you have to put forth the effort.

It is a blessing that my dreams are coming to life; writing acting and most importantly, living.

Keep dreaming and following your dreams, in time they will become your reality.

13
WHAT IS IT ABOUT YOU?

What is it about you that drive women so crazy?
Is it the gaze that you give as you touch their face while you embrace?
Is it your walk, is it your talk?
Is it the cuts in your arms that can do no harm, only hold and console on those lonely nights?

What is it about you that drive women so wild?
You gotta'em acting like a child in a candy store begging for more. You gotta'em so bent that it has left a dent in their bank accounts.
What is it about you that make women do what they do?
Slitting wrists, taking risks…Tattooing backs with no take backs. Paying bills, fixin' the meals…purring like cats as you touch the small of their backs.

Is it the way you slide in between their thighs, touching all highs making them paralyzed screaming for more and more.
Is it that you are hung and that women long to feel and sing the song of ultimate pleasure.
Is it the gentle tug of the hair, the kiss on the neck, the caress of the breast?
Oh, I'm a MESS!!! WHERE'S MY DRESS?!?!

It's not women you drive crazy…IT'S JUST ME! It's those bedroom eyes that gaze at me. It's the way your lips touch my hips as you dip down and low. I grip the sheets 'cause I can't take it anymore.

It's the way you touch my outer pleasures, as well as my inner treasures. It's the roll of your tongue as it strolls down my path of passion, in no form or fashion.

It's the way we fit like glove when we are making love. I don't want this moment to end. It's you and only you that can touch me and take me so high, so high that I feel I can touch the sky.

Sexual intensity is so high that I start to cry, I start to cry because I know all this could not be…if you did not love me. Oh man what is it about you?

14
ONE DAY

They say no love gained, is no love lost; which means no broken hearts or scattered tears. But in reality, love lost is simply unspoken words, shattered dreams and lonely hearts; living life with what if and regrets.

Crying oneself to sleep at night wishing that the hurt would go away, but it never does it just stays, stays for another lonely night and a day of wishful thinking.

The day is on the way for someone to take the hurt away. He is waiting to wipe your tears away and to tell you "Your tears were not in vain…they were just the light to guide me to you."

One day you will not have to cry anymore, unless you are crying tears of joy.
One day you will not have to worry about if you are pretty enough because he will tell and show it to you every day.

I'm still waiting for that day…

15
WHEN DOES MY HEART MEND?

Looking in your eyes, seeing through all your lies.
Pretending that I am mad, hating that the truth is sad
Watching you put me through so much pain, sick and tired of all the rain.

When does this pain end, when does my life begin?
How did it get this far, to the point of where we are?

When did we begin to hate, when did our love dissipate?
The one thing that I know is true, I never really loved you.

I was hooked on your smile and blinded by your charm, but knowing you only meant me harm.

A few months have gone and past, didn't know if it was going to last.
The rain has come to an end, and now my heart can mend.

I know it may seem crazy, but I do wish you the best and as far as the rest,
Well I guess you can say I passed the test.

16
TURN YOUR BACK

When no one else was around I was there for you, but now when I need you, you turn your back on me.

When you needed someone to talk to, I did not turn my back on you.
When you needed someone to lean on, even if you did not take my offer, I did not turn my back on you.
When you needed help with WHATEVER, I did not turn my back.

When I needed someone to lean on, you told me it was too much for you to deal with. You turned your back.

When you needed me, I did not tell you that it was too much for me to deal with. I bent over backwards, sideways, anyways, always to be there for you. And now you turn your back on me.

Okay, so you took me here and you took me there. You gave me money for this, you gave me money for that. You let me stay with you rent free even though I did not ask.
But when I needed you the most, I mean when I REALLY NEEDED you, you turned your back.

You tell me the way I deal with things just does not fit in your lifestyle. Well hell, I did not agree with the way you dealt with stuff. BUT I NEVER, NOT ONCE did I turn my back on you.

You turned your back on me like I was nothing, like I have never done anything for you.

Where would you be if I had turned my back on you?

What would you have done if I told you the same things you told me and turned away?

You told me yourself that I was your last resort. How can you so easily turn your back on me?

17
TIME

If time was something that I could get back, I would rewind back to everyday we argued and I said I hate you or I wish I was never born, the thoughts of wanting another family or even being dead.

If time was something that I could get back, I would take back every time that I made you cry, every time that I disappointed you.

If time was something that I could get back, I would go back to each time you were sick and do everything that I could to make you feel better.

If time was something that I could get back, I would not spend it being mad at you for what my dad did or didn't do. I would spend that time loving you for all the sacrifices you made for me.

If time was something that I could get back, I would go back to December 31, 1998 and I would spend New Year's Eve with you instead of my so called friends.

If time was something that I could get back, I would not waste it trying to be like others or please other people, I would be what God wanted to me to be.

But most importantly, if time was something that I could get back, I would press pause to the day that you died. I would tell you how much I love you.

But since time is something that I cannot get back, I won't waste any more hating myself for the things that I did or didn't do.

I won't waste any more time trying to be someone that I am not.
I won't waste any more time being outside the will of God.
I won't waste any more time with lip service.
As for today and forever, I am going to LIVE!

Live in the present and not in the past,
Live in abundance, full of peace and love,
Live for God and God alone,
Live for today, for tomorrow is not promised and yesterday is already gone

18
THIS IS ME. . .

I love God first and foremost and NO ONE comes before Him!
I cut my nails off just so I can work on my car.
I go six months without getting a perm just because.

My style and dress is whatever I feel best . . . and what I feel best in is a pair of sweats and a t-shirt, or maybe a pair of jeans and a button down.
The whole dress and heels has NEVER been me! But when I do it, Best believe. . . I DO IT WELL!!

Yeah I got a set of "Twinz" but I don't flaunt them because they are not what make me.

I'm not the average girl; I probably turn to a sports game quicker than you. I'll admit, I may not know all the calls or team names but I enjoy watching them. Maybe not baseball, it's too long.

I don't mind paying my way and sometimes your way every now and then . . . just don't make it habit.

I work out for health not to be skinny. . . This is me 5'3 and proud to be a BBW! Why? Because God made me!

This is me, I love hard and I love long.
I cherish the little things like the long talks on the phone or the midday text messages just to see how my day is going.

NOW, DON'T GET IT TWISTED. . I like the 5-star dining and the flashy gifts, but I prefer a man that fears God with a diamond heart.
This is me. You can love me or hate me . . . but I will never stop being me!

19
ONE LAST LETTER

I loved you from the start; you had my heart and tore it apart.
I took the lies, I had my cries. When does the pain end?

When does my heart begin to mend? Was I not enough woman for you?
I guess not cause you had 2 Jennifers, 1 Kim, and only God knows who else.
What did I do for you to give me pleasures beyond measures, then turn around and not even come around for months on end?

Brian McKnight said, 'It's been 6 months, 8 days 12 hours since you went away.' Well you can just double that time and that is how long it's been since you went away.
I thought what we had was good and so right, I guess it was just the heat of the night.

How can you hurt me and love all at the same time?
Am I blind?

Maybe this isn't love, but if it isn't, why do I feel this way?
No matter how hard I try to fight it, I can't deny it…..

I'm so in love with you and it's dangerous. It's dangerous to the point of no return.
It has been said, 'Anything worth having is worth fighting for,' but I don't know who my fight is with.

Is it the other women, is it you, or is it me cause I can't take the hint and let it go.
It's been over a year since I have seen you, but what I feel has not disappeared.
How can you give me so much pleasure and cause me so much pain? Am I the one to blame?

I use to be able to feel you even when you are not around. I use to just think about you and there you would appear.

And now I long to feel you and have you near. I pray that one day you will come back to me.

20
JUST LET HER BE...

You made promises and broke them all, but yet you still try and call.
Come around even when you know she can't stand you to be around.

Just Let Her Be.

You call all the time with 'Baby I'm Sorry' or 'I apologize' but never giving reasons or excuses, not even an explanation about why you did what you did. You've been told not to call and to stay away, but you do both anyway.

The damage has been done to the point where it doesn't matter how many times you say "I'm sorry" or how many stories you tell.
She is not going back and you can't come back.

Just let her be

She just wants to get away….away from the pain, away from the hurt and gain her strength and ease her pain…

Just Let Her Be.

Time has gone and past, but you still can't let go. You call and write and try to plead your case, while she has moved on to a better place.

Just let her be, just let ME be.

21
IT'S NOT THAT EASY

It's not that easy just to let go of someone that you have cared about for so long. It's not that easy to give up someone that you value and cherish so much.

It's not that easy for me to just turn my back and walk away from someone who I tried to make it work with.

It's not that easy for me to say 'the hell with everything.' See it's not that easy for me to give up without fighting. I have been fighting for this long and according to you, I am in it too deep to turn back now.

It's easier for me to try and work things out and deal with the problems that might arise then to just walk away.

Is it that easy for you? If so, why did you wait so long to let me go? Were you through using me or was it not that easy for you?

22
IT AIN'T THE FIRST TIME

It ain't the first time that someone has come into my life and moved me in a way that I have never been moved before, then just have them leave in a blink of an eye.

It ain't the first time that I have had my life turned inside out, upside down and turned all the way around, just for me to land flat on my face.

It ain't the first time I shut people out because of my past, the past that did not last and left me with pain. Pain that has caused me to ruin the present and maybe the future…a never ending cycle that I want to break.

It is the first time that a man came in and didn't have other motives, but because of the past I thought that it wouldn't last, so I shut him out just as fast as he came in.

The pain I'm feeling now is like no other, no other because he was real and true. That was the first time and I hope that was not the last, cause I don't want to pass up or miss out on the joy that I long for and deserve.

23
I WANNA BE LOVED

Something faithful and true

Something real and genuine

I'm sick of all the fake shh….

I wanna be loved for me, I wanna be me 'cause that's all I know how to be.

I wanna be loved, is that too much to ask for?

Someone who will be there, who will care about me, never leave me or deceive me.

I wanna be loved…

Thank You God for loving me.

24
NOW THAT IT'S OVER

Now that it's over, we can't go back to the way things use to be.
We can't go back to the way things should have been.

Now that it's over, can the hurt we caused be mended, can the tears be dried away? No, now that it's over we realized that we have only cause more pain. Now that it's over, what do we do now, what do I do?

You have moved on to another, while I sit and watch.
I have tried to move on, but it seems like it still comes back to you.
Even when I think that I am ok and have moved on, I'm afraid because the road ahead looks like the one before.

Now that it's over, I have cried more tears then I did when we were together. Now that it's over, I sit and think what I could have done different.

Well, now that it's over, I am determined to not make the same mistakes.
I am stronger now that it is over.
I am wiser.
I am a better person.

Now that it's over, now that you're gone, I can now focus on me.
In the end, now that it is over I am on the road to a better me.

25
THE END

After all that has been said and done, we finally have come to an end. I have been feeling it for quite some time now but, I never thought that it would actually end.

I thought my love would be strong enough for the both of us to make things last. But now I know that you don't feel the same way, I know that it has to end no matter how much it hurts.

I guess you and I were never meant to be. I just can't believe things between us have come to an end. Even though I always felt the need to leave, I never thought that I would actually go through with it.

It is time for me to close this chapter in my life; I have been on the same page for far too long. Who knows, maybe you will be part of another chapter in my life.

Maybe this ending could be a new beginning for us, if not I'm glad that we ended in peace.

26
SUICIDE

Suicide…you hear this word and for me and some other people, may think weak minded; taking the easy way out…this is something that I would never have to worry about. Some people think all these things and even more until you are actually faced with it. Whether it be you yourself or someone close to you. For me it was both. Freshman year in High School, I tried to commit suicide. To tell you the truth, I really didn't know much about suicide, I just knew that I wanted all the pain to go away. I was an overweight freshman, pressured to keep my grades up because of the gifted and talented program (GT program) I was in, my mom was up and down with her health, sibling rivalry and too many other issues to name that I had not faced. Little did I know it was the devil trying to stop me from what God planned. Only a couple of people knew what I had done, I wish I could say that this was the only time that I had attempted suicide.

Back in 2000, I tried again. My mom had just passed away in 1999, I was in recovery for my drug and alcohol addiction, my relationship with my dad was strained; ugh just an all-around disaster. But the icing on the cake that set me off was my so called best friend, who was a guy, decided to get married without evening saying anything to me. I know what you are thinking-Why would that set you off? Well, I had more than friendship feelings towards him. He was going through some things and I was there to help. At that time, we had been friends for about 16 years now. You know it really wasn't that he got married, but it was his smug and nonchalant attitude that he had towards the whole thing and the reason he had even gotten married was to make his mother mad. I was just too devastated. Long story short, I spent a week and a day in the behavioral unit at Methodist Hospital.

That was the WORST experience of my life. Being told what to do, when to eat, when to sleep, what to do and what not to do; it was just horrible. But I thank God that I went through it. As I look back over things, especially this last time, I really didn't want to die; I mean I had a loaded gun in my possession, and I didn't use it. Over the next few months I went through therapy, of course they wanted me to get back pills but I refused, I knew God had healed me from being dependant on pills back in 1998. I got myself back in church and tried to live my life.

During the next few years, my dad passed away, than my grandmother, and later on a close friend of mine. Sadly suicide hit home again, only this time it was not me, it was my ex-fiancé.

We use to work together back in 2000, he was my former supervisor. He was actually one of the people that fussed at me when I went through my suicide. He was almost 30 years my senior but we had a special connection, we could talk about anything and everything. During the next few years we discussed a relationship but really never pursued anything because of the age difference. I ended up graduating college and moving to Texas in 2010. It had been over a year since I last talked to him and out the blue I got a phone call from him. We talked like normal, but then he started to get real deep and personal. After he finished all I could say was, "Well, what are you saying?" Then he asked me if I would marry him? I could tell in his voice that he was a little bit disappointed when I told him that I needed some time to think about things.

After I prayed and talked to my Pastor, the next morning I called and told him "YES!" I was so excited…I really did not have a lot a people to celebrate with me in Texas but with the few associates that I did have, I started going to bridal shows and planning. I found my dress, my colors picked out and I even found some really nice invitations and decorations…. I was so happy. I came home a few weeks later to make things official.

It was funny; we were having our first date and planning our wedding at the same time. I ended up moving back home in October of that same year, I should not have left in the first place, but that is another story. My family was happy and was excited for me; I even had my younger sisters getting fitted for their dresses. Everything was looking and going great! But slowly I started to find out things that I should have known before I said yes. Not to go into all the details, but needless to say, I called off the engagement in December. It was best that he focused on dealing with certain things before we continued with our wedding plans.

I will never forget that day. I was doing my clinical to obtain my CNA license. Our mutual friend and I had been trying to contact him. The week before, he had called and spoke to everyone that he felt close to, that was the last time anybody had heard from him. I was on my break and I got a phone call from our mutual friend, I knew that it was not good but I did not know it was this bad. He had told me that his daughter had found him dead… he had committed suicide. I did not know what to do; I could not leave because if I did than I would have a delay in completing my clinical. I only had a few hours left, I just had to keep myself together until then.

When I got to my car I just broke down, I felt so guilty and responsible for what happened. I felt that I was not supportive enough, that I did not do enough to show him that no matter what, I still cared and that I would always be there. I went home, prayed and cried myself to sleep. When I woke up, God had given me so much peace and released me from all the guilt I was feeling. I was assured that there was nothing I could have done and that I did nothing wrong. He left a two page letter, but unfortunately I may never know what it said.

When I tried to commit suicide, I only thought about myself; I never realized the impact that it has on the people who you leave behind; the unanswered questions and the feeling of not doing enough or not being there. I started writing this story back in December of 2011, but I am only able to complete it now because this was part of my life that I was not ready to share with everyone. But then I realized, sharing my story just might save someone else's life.

Suicide is not the answer; NOTHING is worth taking your life. Please know that you will ALWAYS have someone to talk and that you have other options. If you are reading this, please know that I love you, but God loves you more and He will never leave you, nor forsake you. He will never put more on you that you cannot bear, trust me, I am a witness.

27
SOCIETY

Man.... Why is it that society is willing to accept a Full Figure Male (FFM) faster than they do a Full Figure Female (FFF)? I don't understand it, you see all these FFM performers ranging from actors to singers not being PUBLICLY criticized about their weight (key word I said is publicly, who know what happens behind closed doors) and every other day you hear about a FFF not getting a deal because they are overweight.

I mean when are we going to look at an individual for their talents and not their size? I mean look at Gerald Levert, may he rest in peace. This man could BLOW! The Velvet Teddy Bear was one of his nicknames. Besides health reasons, I never heard anything about his weight. Then look at Kelly Price, this SISTAH can roll with the BEST of them. But whether it is true or not, it was reported that her label told her to lose weight because it was damaging her record sales.

Let's look at American Idol, Reuben Studdard big guy with a powerful voice. I cannot think of her name but on last season, a BBW that could sang the roof off, was not given a REAL CHANCE because she did not fit the picture of what American Idol is.

Flava Flav- I am done with this show. This man isn't looking for real love, he looking for some money. You knew good and well, that you cannot see yourself with a BBW, so why put them on the show; to embarrass them, to make fun of them?

I don't care how many of these talk shows go undercover and do these segments on being a Big Person in society. They can never feel what a real big person feels, reason is because they know at the end of the day their weight zips off.

I am so proud of the BBWs that take a STAND when it comes to these record labels and production companies. But it is so sad how many BBWs have REAL talent but majority of the time are type casted as the Fat Friend of the skinny girl or one of the backup singers in a group who uses their voice about as much as they do the lead singer.

For CRYING OUT LOUD...Society do you know what you are doing to these teenagers? See my frustration all started last week. One of my co-workers was telling me that her 13yr old daughter went to the doctor and he told her that she needed to lose 50lbs. I am TELLIN YOU!! If you would see this girl, she is healthy and does not look in ANY WAY OVER WEIGHT!

Not only is there a problem with being a BBW, but is getting MAD CRAZY for the society girls. When I say Society Girls, I mean the ones who society has labeled beautiful and glamorous- Size 0 to 2, Long hair, and always in the camera eye. These girls are seriously DYING TO BE THIN!

What is it going to take for society to STOP labeling what BEAUTY is? Is it gonna take one of the Society Girls, to commit suicide with a note saying "Because of you I am DEAD. My BLOOD is on YOUR HANDS!"

Sometimes I wish that we all were blind. That way we can only base are decisions on that people's personality, not there looks.

Okay I think I am done. . .for NOW!

As a disclosure, this poem was written back in 2008.

28
SEX AND SPORTS

Can you make the wheels in my mind turn like you make my toes curl?

Can you make me sigh with contemplation just as you make me moan with desire?

Does your stimulation process begin and end in the bedroom, or does it END in the bedroom?

Does your tongue work just as good with words as it does with actions, or does it work better?

When the sex is all over and done, can I still tolerate you or did I OVER rate you?

Do you play with my mind like you play on the field, or is all your game playin' strictly HANDS ON?

I need more than just a few quick plays on the field. I need a playbook full of strategies-offense, defense, special teams EVERYTHING.

Are you game? Do you want to be a free agent or have a permanent position on my team?

Will you be the first and only draft pick or do I have to wait around for a couple more rounds?

Is your game only good for the regular season or can you make it to the playoffs-Get AND retain your title?

There's no easy way to win me.

You can't cheat your way to obtain me; no shortcut or quickies either.

See for me, the actual act of sex is like a sport. You work hard during the regular season. If you're good, you make it to the playoffs. Work a little bit harder, a little bit more hustling, but in the end of the playoffs you will either, WIN OR GO HOME!
Cause in the end, I am the REAL GOLD RING, not some replica from

Sports Illustrated that will tarnish.

See, it DOES matter how the game is played.

It is what you do in the OFF season that determines if you will retain your title.

If you don't get this analogy, then you not even in my league.

I'm in the MAJORS. . .You, are still in the little league.

29
REALITY CHECK

It is funny how we say we want one thing but settle for something far so different.

For instance; WOMEN- you say that you want a man who has a good job, takes care of his business, like a man supposed to and loves you and ONLY YOU! BUT then you turn around and settle for that NO GOOD NEGRO that's living off your paycheck and every now and then he goes upside your head just because he had a bad day.

REALITY CHECK!

Men you ask God to send you a woman that is not after your money and can fix a HOT meal! But then you turn around and settle for the one that the only time you see her is payday and the only thing she knows about cooking is the phone numbers to the local carry-out places.

REALITY CHECK!

Why is it that when God sends you EXACTLY what YOU NEED; we don't embrace it because they are not what we are used to...not the right height, not the right weight we turn them away. Or they are exactly what we are used to dating-right height, right weight, all the right features, but because you have been burned in the past, you think it's time for a change. . .

REALITY CHECK!. . . It is NOT THE SAME PERSON!!

How can God bless you with what you need if you keep settling for less? How can God bless you if you only have TUNNEL VISION!?!?

REALITY CHECK!

30
NOT ENOUGH TIME…

Okay, help me understand this . . . why is it that some individuals have all the time in the world to dedicate to their time to everything else BUT God!?!?

They've got time for their jobs, significant others, birthday parties, and the list goes on and on. Don't you know that He is a jealous God?

That job you're working, that car you're washing on Sunday morning, that significant other that you have, and God gave you ALL OF THAT! And just like He gave it to you, He can take it away just as easily!

I am always hearing, " Tomorrow, I get things right" or "I got time" but my favorite is "One day, one day I'll get it right"

PEOPLE PLEASE WAKE UP!!!

TOMORROW IS NOT PROMISED TO YOU!

YOUR ONE DAY IS TODAY!

People please; this world is not going to get any better. I have realized that and I'd rather live my life like there is a God and a new heaven and earth, than live my life like there is not.

Some people are out here right now wondering why they are working two full-time jobs and still cannot make ends meet. Well let me tell you why, YOUR PRIORITIES ARE ALL OUT OF ORDER!

GET IT TOGETHER!

Your TOMORROW could very well be TODAY!

31
LOVE = MUSIC

Love is like music...

You've got your high notes and your low notes

You got moments when everything comes together like a sweet symphony

Then you have your moments when everything sounds like a teenage garage band

You got times when your smiling and other times when you are crying.

Love is like music...

You can hear different beats, but until you hear the right one

Your song will never be complete.

Love is like music...

You'll never give up editing until it is in sync.

Until every note has its place, til every track has been made.

Many songwriters will come and go

But when the right one comes along you will make hit after hit.

Love is like music...

With all the different sounds and rhythms,

There is always going to be that one beat that keeps you on your feet.

Love is like music,

Cause even when you can't stand a song you can't help but to know the words.

Yeah, Love is like music...

Cause there's a melody in your heart that no matter what you do, you can't turn it off.

Love is Like Music.

32
I'LL TAKE MY TIME, WE'LL TAKE IT SLOW

Whether you will admit it or not I know that you have been hurt probably more than once and just like any other human being, you don't want to be hurt again.

So I'll take my time, we'll take it slow. But don't forget, you saw me cry twice which means I have feelings too and because of the kind of world we live in, I have been hurt too and on more than one occasion.

I know there are people out there you want to try your hand at, but don't forget about the one who wants to try her hand too.

If it's meant to be it will be. I mean it took over 2 years for me to finally come around, but I'm here, I won't push and I won't pry. I'll wait and I'll be patience. I don't know if my position intimidates you or even if you question yourself if you are the right person for me because you still have some ways you know you need to work on, but guess what…so do I.

I am not where I should be, but thank God I am not where I use to be and remember, I told you I was intimidated by you at first and I questioned myself was I even good enough for you.

I realized something; I can't impress you with my looks, dress, or style. I might make your head turn but what impresses you the most is if I don't give up and stay focused…right or wrong?

I know you say that you don't have enough time to commit to somebody, but 5 minutes with you feels like months.

So imagine how I felt those few days that I did not see you.
Those times you came to my job and didn't have to, it took all I had in me not to beg you to stay.

But I'll take my time, we'll take it slow. I don't know what the future holds, but good or bad, I won't be mad because at least I know I have someone I can call friend and hopefully you can do the same.

I can't promise you that everything is going to be easy. I can't promise you that I will get things right. I won't even begin to promise you that I am going to get rid of all my tomboy ways. But I will promise you this, whatever it is that God has ordained me to do and whatever role God has placed me in your life to be, I will do it to the fullest!

If it is to be a friend, I will do my best to be there when you need. To have a shoulder to cry on when times are hard, to be an encouragement or give an encouraging word when you are down. To give an ear when you just need someone to listen.

If it is to be that significant other, I will be all that a friend is and much more. And if I am only here for a season, I will thank God for the time that He has given me with you.

As I sit here, I am debating whether or not to show this to you now, later, or not at all. Should I post this as a blog or just keep it to myself.

Will it push him away, Will it scare him off, or will it bring him closer and ask me to stay?

I don't know what happened the day we first met, but you have been in my spirit since then.

You have been on my mind for months and on my heart for weeks. My walls are down, now can you take down yours?

All I know is that I will be patient, I'll take it slow and we'll take our time. I'll wait but please don't make me wait too long.

33
I KNEW THAT IT WOULD NEVER WORK

As bad as I wanted it to, I knew that it would never work.
We tried but we didn't try hard enough.

The more we tried to deny the past, focus on the future and making things work, the more messed up things got.

I told you in the beginning that it would never work no matter how hard we tried to make it work.

But you wanted to try and I felt it was something worth trying for, even though I knew I was setting myself up for failure.

I knew it would never work, but despite what I knew, I tried anyway.
Maybe if we both tried harder maybe it would have worked.

Then again, maybe we were not meant to have worked.

Yeah most of the times we shared were cool, but we had our moments. Obviously those moments outweighed the good for the both of us…I told you it would never work.

34
HITMAKER

Where is the real hitmaker at?

When is he gonna compose the melody of my heart?

Instead of sitting here wondering why does it hurt so bad,

I got up and decided that good things comes to those who wait.

Instead of asking how could an angel break my heart,

I realize that if he really was an angel he would not have broken my heart in the first place.

Instead of playing another sad love song,

I'm playing the rhythm of life.

The beats that will get me moving cause I'm marching to a different drummer now.

I'm so sick of these songs nowadays...they have no heart.

Gimme that ol' school sound that comes from the soul.

I'm tired of these little drummer boys pretending.

Forget Gold....I am looking for the hitmaker that knows PLATINUM when he sees it.

I don't need no one hit wonders...

I'm looking for a hitmaker that I can enter into a lifetime contract wit.

I am looking for someone that I can make this CD called LIFE a #1 seller.

I'm done with DEMOS,

I'm ready to put it on wax!

We in this THANG TOGETHER,

So you can be like Diddy and be all up in my videos.

And in the end,

We'll write the GREATEST love song that's ever been sold.

Image courtesy of Herman Trass

35
HAVE YOU EVER LOVED?

Have you ever loved someone so much that you knew for sure that you were meant to be?

Have you ever loved someone so hard that your heart breaks when that person is not around?

Have you ever loved someone so much that you would sacrifice your last and even yourself to be sure that they were safe?

But have you ever loved someone so much that others say "You are so in love, It's written all over your face."

But was that really love, if the other person didn't show the same in return. They didn't sacrifice for your safety; their heart didn't break when you were away.
Because you laid down or you were looking at the outer man, what you thought was love was really lust.

Now that you see the inner man, you are in pure disgust.

Love is 1 Corinthians 13:4-8a (NIV)…
Love is patient, love is kind. It does not envy, it does not boast, it is not proud. It does not dishonor others, it is not self-seeking, it is not easily angered, it keeps no records of wrongs. Love does not delight in evil but rejoices with the truth. It always protects, it always trusts, always hopes, always perseveres. Love never fails.

If you don't believe me…READ YOUR BIBLE.

36
GONE TOO SOON...

Let me first start off by saying that I believe in God. I know that everything works together for the good of them that love the Lord. I also know that everything happens for a reason and that at times when I don't understand or feel something is not right, I still trust God. I understand that there was nothing that I could have done to change things because in the end it was all part of God's plan. What I am about to write are just some thoughts I have had recently and in the past about the people that I have loved and have been called home to be with God. These thoughts are very personal and dear to me.

As I write them all down, I often find myself fighting back the tears and other times I just let them flow. I hope that by sharing my experiences someone else will find comfort in know that they are not alone and God is a Comforter. Be encouraged and be blessed.

As I sit here and think about the people that have come in and out of my life, I wonder if they were gone too soon. I wonder if there was something that I could have done to keep them around just a little bit longer. I ask myself if I could have said something different, if I could have done something differently. When I have these moments, the first person that comes to my mind is my mother. For years I wondered if I had never left the room would she still be around. My mom was my rock...there was so much that I wish I had told her so much that I wish she could have seen me accomplish. At times I felt cheated. Then I realize that as much as it hurts, I was being selfish. My mom endured a lot, especially her last few months; amputation after amputation after amputation, her body just could not take it anymore. I know that God used her even until her last breath to be a testimony, to bring souls to Christ. It was a blessing, she may not have known who I was, but she still knew God and was preaching hope and faith, until she could not speak anymore. She had a bucket of mustard seeds in little plastic bags and would pass them out to the staff on her floor. I know from her life and her faithfulness, several people were saved, with this act of faith. My mom was and still a major part of who I am. Her passing was really hard on me, but the impact that she made on other people lives outweighed all that. I have learned that her legacy will forever live on; through lives that she has touched and through me.

Then there is my uncle. He passed away when I was about 6. My uncle was about 6'2, had an afro and a full beard (sometimes). He never did anything wrong to me, always treated me with love and compassion, but because I was young and stupid I thought my uncle was the wolf man and I was scared of him. There would be times that he would try and pick me up or hold me and I would cry. When he passed away, I felt so bad. I loved my uncle, I loved him then and I love him now. But for years I felt that he died not knowing that I loved him. For years I prayed that he understood that I was just a kid and that I did not mean any harm. BUT GOD…He gave me peace and assurance that my uncle understood and knew that I loved him.

My granddad….as the youngest grandchild, my grandfather could not pronounce or write my name, he always called me LaShanta, lol. I was "papa's" baby. There was nothing my grandfather would not have done for me. I was about 10 when he passed away. The day he passed away, we had just left the hospital. We were in the house for less than 10 minutes when we got the phone to come back to the hospital because he took a turn for the worse. Just a few weeks prior, him and my grandmother celebrated their wedding anniversary, unfortunately they had to celebrate while my grandfather was in the hospital.

Sadly, my grandfather was the first that I had to sit in the hospital with. While my grandfather was taking his last breath, my grandmother was on the other side of the hospital in the ER having a heart attack.

My grandmother outlived her husband and both her children. Until this day, I still don't know why and I have come to the understanding that I may never know. My grandmother was beautiful; she was a fighter, and a survivor. I am so glad to have had her in my life. Not only did she survive breast cancer (double mastectomy) but she was also on dialysis for almost 10 years. The average time is 5-6 years. It really upset me to watch my grandmother go through certain things, to watch certain people, including people that call me themselves family take advantage of her. But she was strong, her faith was strong and she kept fighting until God said it was enough and called her home.

I have been blessed to have a man want to give me his last name. No not my husband, my dad, my dad that raised me. From the time I was six months, I called him my dad. When I was 8, I added his last name. I may not have been his, be accepted me like I was his own. He never made a difference between me and his biological children. In fact, the entire Weems family accepted me and my sister and my family got bigger. So when he passed away, it was exceptionally hard. Controversy aside, it was only a couple of years before that my mom had passed away. I was still struggling with my sobriety and was not fully back in church. Before his passing, I had to watch him from a distance. I never really got a chance to say goodbye or that I loved him, but I know he knew. Even as I write this, I cry, I cry because I wish he was here, but I know that he is in a better place.

I now know that even though at one point I thought these individuals were gone to soon, I know they lived their lives to the fullest.

37
EX-LOVERS TRYING TO BE FRIENDS

I use to wonder why I never tried to be friends with an ex-lover…now I know why, it only brings more pain.

Trying to be friends after being lovers is going backwards.
If we could only have been friends first, maybe we could have been lovers and whatever comes after and in between.

I can't be your friend because it only brings pain, pain that I helped cause so you are not fully to blame.

I can't just sit around while you find another when I know that if we were friends first, you would not have to search.

I sit in a daze while you talk to your friend, your potential lover and maybe even your future queen and it hurts me so bad to hear or watch because I know you and I may never be.

We laugh, we joke, and play around but soon that day will come around that it will all end.

Instead of prolonging the pain, I try to end it now.

It hurts like hell, but why wait because it will come anyway and be even more painful. Before the physical love between us was there, the like and sense of love from me was there for you.

You never knew it, but I did. I tried to show and express but I went about it in all the wrong ways.

Once again, all I feel is the pain.

The love is there, but it is only going one way and it is not mine.
Maybe it was just sex to you and maybe it wasn't, but we both know that we did things the wrong way.

I guess all there is left to say is goodbye.
Goodbye to love and I hope she makes you happy, whoever she maybe because I know that it ain't me.

38
DON'T CRY FOR ME –
FOR THE SERVICEMEN AND WOMEN

No one forced me to be here, I chose to come here
Don't cry for me,

Yeah I've seen some things that the average man can't stand, but don't cry for me. It's not by chance or circumstance that I'm here, it's God's plan for me, so don't cry for me.

I'm here so you can stay free,
This is my destiny, so don't cry for me.
God is the controller of my life, He holds me and everyone here is in His hands. Don't cry for me…

As time comes to an end, we know that there is a time for war and a time for peace….this is the time for war.

After I have endured all the tests, after I have seen enough and I have done my best…

God will call me home to rest and say, 'Well done my good and faithful servant.' Don't cry for me, Pray for me.

I slept with the dead so I could stay alive.
I killed so we could live.

I'm proud to be a Solider, a Specialist, a Fighter, a Hero but most of all I am proud to be a Child of God.
So don't cry for me.

I have gone days without sleep, but God restored me and He carried me. Don't cry for me….

My body maybe bruised and scarred, but my spirit and soul is at peace. Don't cry for me…

I fight so you won't have to. If I die today it is so you can live tomorrow. Don't cry for me…God is in control and I will not leave here until God calls me near… So don't cry for me.

39
DEAR MAMA....

Dear Mama,

I just wanted to tell you that I love and miss you. You were there for me when I needed you and I thank you. Some children were not as fortunate as me to have such a loving and caring mother.

It's going to be hard for me to go on but I know you are still watching over me even more because you are in heaven. It's just not the same. I can no longer run to you with my problems. I can't hold you when you are in pain, but that's ok because you no longer have any.

I wish we had more time together. You were supposed to see me get my college degree. You were supposed to be there for my wedding day. At the end of my pregnancy, you were supposed to walk me up and down the stairs because your grandchild was running late and had not come yet. Now that won't happen. I am not selfish though, you were tired and in pain. Now you have gone to a better place where you can be joyful and without pain.

I love you mama and I know that you loved me and I am going to miss your pretty face, but I know you will always be there for me whenever I need you and I will always be your Shanee-Na-Nee.

Love Your Baby Girl....

40
CENTER OF LIFE

The day has finally arrived, the day two became one.
Wedding bells and wedding bands, looking forward to spending the rest of my life with the man that was made for me.

As the scene changes to our honeymoon, I stand here in the candlelight glow, Only wearing what I was born into the world in, I feel the warmth of another, my lover, touching my bare skin.

I turn and see you. I look into your soft brown eyes and I'm all smiles.
The cars and other noise that play outside, we pay it no mind because what we feel right now inside is the only thing we hear.

Feeling each other; our souls, our hearts beating as one.
As you kiss the small of my back, your tongue takes a sensual and exotic journey up my spine. As husband and wife, we make love.

Then something is wrong, everything is not fine.
It was all a dream, a dream that I wish I hadn't woke up from.
You and I were never one and maybe never will be.

No wedding, no wedding bands…no you.

The security that I found in you, someone else has.
I'm not your wife; someone else is the center of your life.

It all felt so real, now my heart needs to heal.
Maybe that is my destiny….
To go through life without being the center of any man's life.

41
CAPTIVATED

I don't know you, but from the first day I saw you, you have captivated me. Dirty clothes, black skully looking quite scummy, but your smile is what got me.

Soft spoken, shy guy is what you are. I don't know why, but you have captivated me. Working hands and working mind, makes me curious to know what else is there to find.

Young, dumb and full of….Well you know the rest.
Young, Yes…Dumb, not by far.

Intellectual, intelligent brotha that has caught my eye.
I don't know much about you , but I hope to go deeper, deeper into your mind to find what else is behind those brown eyes.

Those brown eyes that are a window to someone I want to get to know, those brown eyes that are a window to what I only can see is a pure soul. Since the day I met you, you have been a topic, a topic of interest, a topic of curiosity, a topic of amazement.

Even though it has been said 'curiosity killed the cat,' but I believe that satisfaction brought it back.

If I have to judge by looks, you are off the hook. Brown skin, slim and trim with eyes that tend to make me melt like butter. A smile that is a mile long that shines like sun on clear summer's day. You have captivated me.

I want to know more, open doors to who you are. I want to know for sure that it is not the outer appearance that has me here.

I'm like a kid on Christmas morning; I want to open up the pretty package to see what is really inside.

Will it be the new outfit I was eyeing at the store or another pair of tube socks from grandma?

I am intrigued by you and I want to get to know you…you have captivated me.

42
BEHIND THESE BROWN EYES

Behind these brown eyes there are secrets waiting to be told.
These eyes have seen things that only some people can imagine.

Can you see behind these brown eyes?
Do you see the pain, the hurt, the fears?
Do you see the heartache and the failures?

Look deeper, there are more to these brown eyes….
There is love, a love so deep that it burns to be free.

There is peace, the kind of peace that one can only get from God.
No, you don't see. You are blinded by what the world tells you to see.

Behind these eyes there is power…power to change.
Do you see the dreams and the hopes for the future?

There is strength…strength to overcome anything and all obstacles.
But most of all there is Love

Love to Heal, Love to Feel, Love to Grow
Love to cover a multitude of sin.
Love that holds no debt.
Love that loves in spite of not being loved in return.
Can you see behind these eyes?
Can you see into these eyes?

43
A MOTHER

A mother is a friend when no one else is around.
A mother is a shoulder to cry on when things seem to look grim.
A mother is someone who will always be there for you even when you are in the wrong.

She will stand by your side until it was all over and if it turned out bad, she would always be there to tell you everything will be okay.

A mother is the first person that you bound with. She will guide you and try to show you the right things to do. She will teach you things that she has learned.

She will show and tell you her mistakes so that you won't make them.

On June 28, 1999 my mother was called from labor to reward. It hurts even until today, but I know she is not suffering anymore.

A mother's love and spirit still lives when their physical presence is gone.

44
A CHANCE

I use to wish for another chance, now I wish for just a chance.

A chance to be your friend, a chance to be your lover, a chance to be the woman that you want and need.

All in that order, not one before another. We never had a chance to be something really true, because we did one before another.

Now all I ask is for a chance for us to mend the tears that have been made and try to go on.

A chance for us to love again, but now I see that chance will never come and the rips maybe permanent.

45
NOW HOW DOES IT FEEL?

Now that I am gone how does it feel?
Was I really the one that was causing your problems?
Or was I the one that was making things better for you?

Let's see you've been married, divorced, married again and now divorced again, but according to you, I was your headache.

So tell me now, how does it feel?

I supported your dreams and your goals, I encouraged you to keep going, but you still chose to walk away.
Years later, you still in the same position…ALONE.
What happened to the 'realest female you ever met'?

Now how does it feel that the REALEST female was the one you left behind?
The one who stood by you when you had nothing, who sacrificed what she had so you wouldn't be without, how does it feel now that I am gone?

How does it feel, now that you see that the grass was not as green as you thought?

Now how does it feel when you see me the one you left behind, stronger and better now that you are not around to hold me back? I've got my thang going on, writing checks that I only dreamed of doing because I use to be so focused on you.

Yeah, it's cool that you woke up, apologized and tried to make things right. I appreciate that you admitted it was all you and that it was your fault, you pushed me away. But sorry boo, you left your mark, the damage was done and now I am not the same. I am stronger and wiser, oh yes; I have forgiven you but I am not falling for the OKEY DOKE again…

Moral of the story…be careful with what you say, words hurt just as much as a fist, and can cause just as much pain. Life and death is in the power of the tongue.

46
RAPE

It was my fault; maybe if I had not skipped school, maybe if I was not smoking weed this would not have happened.

Was it really rape? He didn't hit me, I have no bruises...but several times I said STOP, I tried to get up.

I'm a virgin, I did not want my first time to be like this; I was saving myself for marriage. Maybe it was a dream. No, the pain reassures me that this is real.

Will my friends believe me? ... Do I believe me?

What will my best friend think, what will he do? It was his cousin that raped me. I'm just a friend; he will probably take his side.

Did I ask for this 'cause I kissed him back?

Did he use a condom? What if I am pregnant? What if he gave me some disease? What am I going to do? ...Is my life now over!

Should I tell my parents? What would I say… "Mom, when I was skipping school and smoking weed and I was raped."

What would she think of me; the disgrace and disappointment? If, I had never put myself in the situation, this would have never happened… It was my fault, I deserved it.

I am so ashamed and I will take this to the grave…

In my junior year in high school, while skipping school and under the influence of marijuana, I was raped; date rape or acquaintance rape to be exact. At that time, I thought a rape victim had to beaten up to be considered rape or if she did not know the person; I knew almost nothing about date rape. I was so afraid and ashamed.

As I have gotten older, I have come to realize that it was not my fault and I should have spoken up. No matter what you are wearing or if you are intoxicated, if you said 'No,' and did not want it to happen, than it should not have.

Being raped takes a part of you, but you can get that part of you back, it took me some time, but I got mine back. No longer am I a victim. I forgave him but most importantly, I forgave myself, it's funny, forgiving him was easier than forgiving myself.

Speak up and know that you are not alone. Even though it may feel like your life is over, it is not, and you can be a survivor just like me.

47
SIBLINGS

I have been blessed to have a HUGE family. Not including all the people that I have adopted, I have a total of 12 other siblings, yep 12. My dad has 6, my mom had 1but her first husband had 3 other, and my dad that raised me had 3 from his first marriage. I was only raised in the house with my one sister but my other siblings have always been around and I love them ALL!

For the most part of my life, I had been the baby. Boy I tell you, growing up with older siblings was no joke; one of my brothers, knocked my tooth out during a pillow fight, I will never forget that day.

Having a blended family brings its challenges but we have overcome them. We never used the term 'step' or 'half'; it was ALWAYS brother or sister; a difference was never made. I may not talk to them as much, but I know that I can call on them anytime and they can call on me.

After so many years of being the little sister, I am now able to be the big sister and having two little sisters under me is a HUGE task. I see so much of me in them and when I talk or tell them things it's only because I don't want them to make the same mistakes as I did. They currently live the closest to me and we get to hang out.

From the youngest to the oldest, the nearest to the farthest, I love my siblings. We may cuss and fuss, but in the end we always agree to disagree.

From Sunrise to Sunset : A Poetic Journey

48
ABOUT THE AUTHOR

Nashanta Taylor-Weems was born and raised in Gary, Indiana. A product of the Gary Community School Corporation, she graduated from Theodore Roosevelt High School in 1997. She later graduated from Ivy Tech Community College with her Associate's in Computer Science and Business Management. In May 2009, she graduated from Trine University in Angola, Indiana with a Bachelor's of Science in Psychology and a Bachelor's of Applied Management in Business. She is currently pursuing her Master's degree. At one point in time to be able to say that she was a college graduate, almost seemed impossible, so for her it is truly a blessing and an accomplishment.

Ms. Taylor-Weems, attends True Faith Church Ministries which is located in Gary, Indiana and has been under the leadership of Pastor Anthony Goffin Sr. for over 13 years. As the Singles Ministry Leader and member of the praise team, Ms. Taylor-Weems, counts it all joy for EVERYTHING that she has experienced! Please don't look at her as a victim because she is not, she is Victorious! As painful as some of these experiences have been, they all made her into the woman that she is today; she is a Living Testimony.

www.ingramcontent.com/pod-product-compliance
Lightning Source LLC
Chambersburg PA
CBHW041641090426
42736CB00034BA/2